Reviews

"De Avila's fascinating journey includes reassuring and encouraging correspondence so characteristic of my late father, a remarkable man committed to helping others discover the gifts within themselves."

Joni Treffert Stine
Fond du Lac, Wisconsin

"Diana de Avila has experienced injury, illness and adversity, yet continued to move forward. A recurrence of illness, which could have proved a setback, instead brought a gift that has translated into an impressive body of artwork. In *Soldier, Sister, Savant*, the reader is provided insight into Ms. de Avila's journey and navigation to a new reality."

Donald Higgins, M.D.
Chief Physician Educator, National Center for Patient Safety
Veterans Health Administration
Professor of Neurology, Albany Medical College

"Sometimes we spend a lifetime trying to find our talents, and sometimes our talents find us. This is the story of Diana de Avila, an extraordinary woman with an extraordinary gift and a heart full of resilience."

Mafer Bencomo
Documentary filmmaker and Ringling College and Design student
https://vimeo.com/maferbencomo

"After recounting Diana de Avila's early careers as a soldier, nun, and successful business woman, Dr. Wilma Davidson and Diana delineate her processes and accomplishments as a visual artist savant induced by multiple sclerosis and a prior traumatic brain injury. A unique and important contribution to the literature on a creative phenomenon."

Janet Emig, Ed.D.
Professor Emerita, Rutgers University
DHL from Mt. Holyoke College as a Distinguished Alumna
Honorary Doctorate from Monmouth University for service in the teaching of writing

"The only thing more fascinating than Diana de Avila's visually stunning artwork is the story of how she came upon her rare talent. This artist's journey is one of challenges met and overcome. *Soldier, Sister, Savant* provides an engaging, personal look into the little-known world of acquired savant syndrome and a deeper understanding of how Diana's amazing artwork is born."

Dr. Clay Montcastle, Director
Virginia War Memorial

"Works created by most savants have an engaging style and gift containing the key to a beauty most of us can't perceive. However, de Avila's body of work brilliantly bridges the gap while offering visually sumptuous and compelling works that demand to be examined and understood."

Tim Jaeger
painter

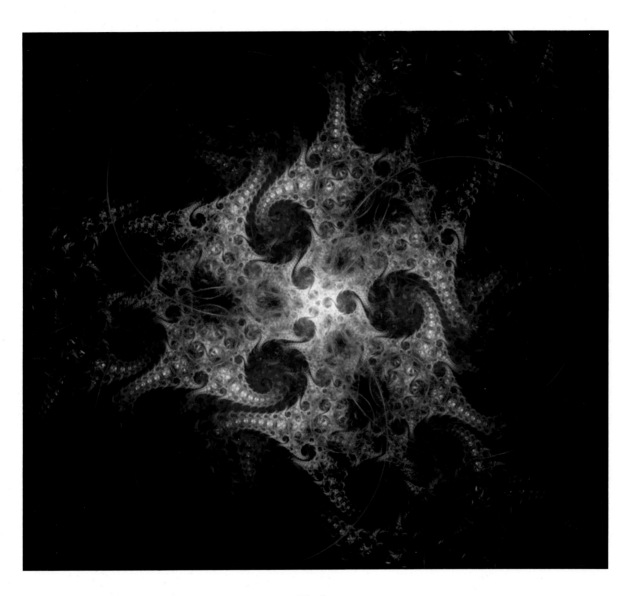

Hydra
Diana de Avila

Soldier,

Sister,

Savant

Cover art and design: Diana de Avila
Book layout and design: Diana de Avila and Lucy Arnold

Editor: Nancy Dafoe

ISBN 978-1-950251-00-1 (paperback)
ISBN 978-1-950251-02-5 (eBook)

Library of Congress Control Number: 2021905675

First edition
Printed in the United States of America

Published by
The National League of American Pen Women, Inc.
PEN WOMEN PRESS

Founded in 1897,
The National League of American Pen Women, Inc.
is a nonprofit dedicated to promoting the arts.
1300 17th Street NW
Washington, D.C. 20036-1901
www.nlapw.org

Soldier, Sister, Savant

Wilma Davidson, Ed.D.
Diana de Avila, M.S.Ed.

Pen Women Press

Dedication

For
Jake, Ian, Ben, and Emily
From Wilma Davidson

For
CC
From Diana de Avila

To laugh often and much;

To win the respect of intelligent people
and the affection of children;

To earn the appreciation of honest critics
and endure the betrayal of false friends;

To appreciate beauty;
To find the best in others;

To leave the world a bit better, whether by
a healthy child, a garden patch
or a redeemed social condition;

To know even one life has breathed
easier because you have lived;

This is to have succeeded.

by Ralph Waldo Emerson

Acknowledgments

Wilma Davidson and Diana de Avila thank and acknowledge Lucy Arnold of Pen Women Press and our PWP editor Nancy Dafoe, both of whom responded with apt suggestions, remarkable enthusiasm, and an energy that refueled us.

Additionally, we acknowledge Dr. Berit Brogaard, a brain researcher who studies savantism and synesthesia, who answered our queries with immediate interest when we contacted her "out of the blue" and generously agreed to conduct further research on Diana's "accidental gift;" the late Dr. Darold Treffert, an international expert on savantism, who identified Diana's unique condition; and Dr. Keith Rafal, a rehabilitative physician whose organization, Our Heart Speaks, provides a resource for those with chronic illness and new disability to share their personal stories of meaning and hope.

The authors thank each other: "Without Diana, her friendship, her grit, and her gift of art, I would have no story to write."

"Without Wilma and her ability to express my thoughts with such precision, I would remain silent inside my art."

*

Additionally, Wilma Davidson expresses her gratitude to Dr. Janet Emig, her doctoral mentor, "who believed in me before I believed in myself, and who taught me what I know about writing."

She also expresses her deepest thanks, "to family who put up with my compulsiveness about everything and love me regardless. Thank you to friends and colleagues who graciously listened to ideas and willingly read the drafts with encouragement and praise; and to any and all who have endured serious injury who may find this story inspirational; to those involved in the research, medical, and rehabilitative community who may want to know more about how the brain rewires itself; and to all who are open and curious and believe all things are possible."

*

Diana de Avila extends her gratitude to the doctors and medical teams at the Michael Bilirakis DVA Spinal Cord Injury (SCI) Center at the James A. Haley Veterans' Hospital who provided extraordinary care and a supportive path forward; to Dr. Neil Lava who first diagnosed her multiple sclerosis and "helped me understand that this diagnosis was not an end, and that my path forward was up to me; to the Daughters of Saint Paul, especially Sr. Julia Mary Darrenkamp and Sr. Rose Pacatte who have been sisters in the truest sense of the word; to the U.S. Army, Falconer, and my sisters and brothers in Charlie 10 where we quickly discovered that life and obstacles 'ain't nothing but a thing.'"

"I also thank Walt, who helped me to dream and believe anything was possible; Rosie and Diana, my inspiration for my military aspirations; Colette, my closest high school friend and band buddy. You will always hold a special place in my heart. And to my family and friends who stayed the course with me, believed in me, and watched me navigate life's curveballs."

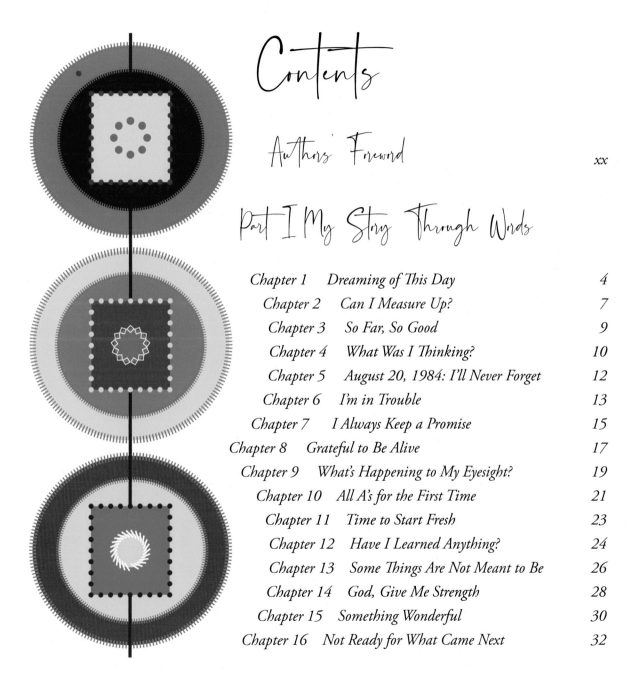

Contents

Authors' Foreword

I met Diana de Avila early in 2020 while volunteering for the local branch of a national, non-profit, interdisciplinary arts organization for women and was immediately engaged by her bubbly personality, ever-present smile, and genuine kindness. I was also drawn to Diana because she had been diagnosed with a medical condition similar to that of a member of my family.

We bonded immediately and have become the best of friends. You know, the kind of friend you feel you have known all your life. The kind of friend who can read your mind, understand your brand of spirituality, and share a compulsiveness just like your own.

As a writer, with the obsessive streak just mentioned, I was compelled to let others know about this incredible woman. And so, with Diana's blessing, as well as her countless hours sharing her life story, I was able to become Diana's voice, tell her tale, offer her words.

This account covers the significant events in her life that led her to where she is today. *Soldier, Sister, Savant* narrates the mystery and pain surrounding her journey, her can-do attitude, her unflinching faith in the Almighty, and her inspirational spirit in the face of life-threatening odds. Others would have lost hope, despaired, and given up, but not Diana. She made art. I am grateful that she let me deliver her words here.

May you also find inspiration in her and her story, just as I do!

Wilma Davidson, Ed.D.

My life, as you will soon discover, has been full of unexpected twists and turns, and I've been told that I should write a book about it.

Almost, as if by magic, I met Wilma Davidson through the Sarasota Branch of the National League of American Pen Women (NLAPW). Wilma was a branch officer at the time I was applying for NLAPW membership and presenting my work to the board members. It was a winter day in 2020, and I remember feeling like a stranger in a strange world when I applied to become an art member of this national, professional women's organization. That day, Wilma met me with a ready smile, putting me at ease right away. I could tell through the sincerity in her eyes and her almost negligible New England accent that there was going to be a bond between us.

I was right. Since then, which feels like many years condensed into one, our lives have intersected daily as we have moved from acquaintances to lifelong friends. We share our mutual admiration and artistic gifts with each other and work together at warp speed, with a complementary interaction only we can understand. We condense days into hours and weeks into days. It is the energy in our in-sync industry that makes me feel as if there isn't anything we can't accomplish as a duo.

My life, which was already blessed despite many obstacles, is better with Wilma in it. And I am thankful that she can be my words whenever I need them. A rare find!

This adventure of sharing my life and art with her has been both exciting and cathartic. I am thankful for where I've been and for where I'm going. I feel blessed to be able to share my story with you now.

Diana de Avila, M.S.Ed.

Glitter Bomb

Diana de Avila

Part I

My Story Through Words

"The meaning of life is to find your gift.
The purpose of life is to give it away."
by Pablo Picasso

Enfoldment
Diana de Avila

Chapter 1
Dreaming of This Day

Are we here?

The bus had stopped. I glanced at my watch; it was 11:30 a.m. We'd been riding for two and a half hours, following a twenty-three-hour train ride. I was nearly a thousand miles away (really, 746 miles) from my home in Rockville, Maryland. The bus was hot, my clothes wrinkled, and my shoes heavier than cement that September day.

My just-turned-eighteen-year-old self, wanting to show my zeal, popped up from my seat.

I want them to see me motivated right from the start. I've got to hide my shy and naturally contemplative self.

I pulled my suitcase and my sixty-pound duffel down from the overhead rack and headed toward the front of the bus, the way any teenager might, trying discreetly to get in closer to the front of the line while other passengers were still gathering their gear. Having just turned right toward the open bus door, I was ready to exit, to descend the steps onto pavement, and share my excited but introverted self with those there to greet me. But something happened.

Oh, no!

My suitcase lodged itself sideways in the open-door space as I tried to exit.

Crap, this is too embarrassing! I've been dreaming of this day since I was in eighth grade.

This isn't supposed to be how my entrance unfolds.

The bus driver leaned over as I tried to unwedge the suitcase and said, "If you can make it through the next twenty-four hours, honey, you'll be okay."

I was beginning to have doubts, but my suitcase relented, and all five-foot-nine-inches of me, with suitcase in tow, finally and ungracefully was separated from the bus.

I'm in the Army now! Oh, boy.

I was on the grounds of Fort McClellan, Alabama, which was to be my home for the next five months. I and the rest of the bus-full of recruits were greeted by Drill Sergeant Duncan, who immediately told us to hold our IDs up in the air for what seemed like infinity. Little did I know that he was, by comparison, a gentle precursor to a second drill sergeant, who was nightmare scary.

I kid you not.

I learned instantly that my cheerful demeanor, my bubbly though shy disposition, and eternal smile were not a welcome greeting for a drill sergeant.

But I wasn't deterred. I had always been patriotic, thanks to my mom and dad, who was from Bolivia, and both of whom imparted an authentic love of the United States of America and the Almighty in me. I talked so much about serving my country when I was in high school that I even convinced four classmates to join! But in those first moments in the presence of these drill sergeants, I did have to remind myself that joining the Army was all my idea.

Be careful what you wish for, girl. Where's my three-minutes-older-than-me-twin brother when I need him?

Diana de Avila at eighteen

Chapter 2
Can I Measure Up?

During the earliest days there, I learned how to salute, do push-ups on demand, and maintain enough strength to keep my dream of serving my country alive. Yes, I even did the "Pit," a term expressing the dreaded activity of diving into a pool-like pit made of dirt with a concrete base, pumping out ten push-ups, crab-walking the pit's length (about thirty feet) and, at the end, turning around and digging a trench the whole way back with my forehead.

Military Operations in Urban Terrain (MOUT) training was a second test of my endurance. Using grappling hooks, I had to find ways to scale walls and get into windows of our simulated urban environment (which, at that time was just an empty wooden structure). These drills and more were part of basic training.

Initially, I wanted to join a medical unit, but those hopes were quickly dashed because no openings in the med unit existed. So, I chose what I thought would be almost as exciting: 95B Combat Military Police (MP).

Being a Lady Cop sounded cool, huh?

As quiet as I was, I had always liked excitement.

By far, the most grueling challenge of my MP training was the obstacle course that tested all the resolve I had. In retrospect, that tough training likely prepared me for what life had in store.

The MP obstacle course was a test of getting over any fear of heights and having the strength needed to hang on for dear life. There were no safety harnesses at that time, and if a soldier fell from a high obstacle, it was dire.

All the training was grueling and exhausting. Only two-thirds of the women who started training with me finished with my unit. Some went home and others were sent to new units and recycled to start training all over again. This set-back happened to my close Army buddy, and I was heartbroken. There were times when, after being on night duty until wee hours, I was up again at 3:45 a.m. More than once, I found myself putting on a second bra over one I had already donned as I tried to function on little-to-no sleep. Luckily, I remembered my mantra about service to the country I loved and often wrote home about my exploits.

I was determined to give this my all.

Turns out, I almost did.

Chapter 3
Sr Fav. Sr Grrd

Months later, after making it through one station unit training (OSUT), I was sent to my first duty station, Hunter Army Airfield in Savannah, Georgia. At eighteen and still naïve, I thought about auditioning for the Army Band. I was musically oriented, played several instruments, and had loved any high school class that ended in band: marching band, concert band, jazz band. I also loved wearing the uniforms!

Darn! I blew it.

I managed to get an appointment to audition, and I also managed to sleep through my audition. But instead of going after it again and fulfilling that dream, I decided to go through psych and stress testing to get ready for counter terrorism/hostage rescue training. After weeks of intense training with FBI, CIA, military, and law enforcement personnel, I graduated third in my class as the only female.

Yes, and I still have the cheeky certificate signed by every one of my twenty-six all-male SWAT team brothers!

That special reaction team (SRT)/SWAT training was the highlight of my army career and the most challenging accomplishment in my life, up to that point.

Little did I know then about real challenges.

Chapter 4
What Was I Thinking?

After my initial SWAT training, I was motivated and psyched to take on the next challenge: Advanced Special Reaction Team training.

I got to go home first and enjoy a vacation out of uniform and prepare for the next adventure, which would include advanced hostage negotiations and rescue tactics.

Time home allowed me to be with my boyfriend at that time, who soon became my fiancé. He was one of those people I had talked into going into the Army, and since he was several years older than me, he had already made it through his training and was at his new duty station.

I remember when we headed to a special military function in Washington, D.C., both wearing our Army Class A uniforms. He was driving his Datsun, and there was a box of Cracker Jacks lying in the center console. I loved Cracker Jacks, and I especially loved those little collectible prizes. He asked me to open the Cracker Jack box, and I went straight for the prize. He knew me well. My crafty boyfriend had managed to put a diamond ring inside the sealed box of Cracker Jacks!

I said, "Yes!" We spent some wonderful time in Lake George, New York. I loved the diamond. I felt so grown up! Eighteen and engaged!

After that exciting time off, I returned to base for more advanced training. I wanted to work on Australian rappelling. In our case, we would be doing it upside down.

What was I thinking?

Chapter 5
August 20, 1984: I'll Never Forget

Recently returned from a vacation to see family and newly engaged, I was on my friend's borrowed motorcycle traveling through our barrack's long parking lot.

Oh, God, no! I have no foot brakes! No hand brakes!

I had to find a way to stop myself before I ran into traffic.

Screech! Dear God, please.

Going just over forty miles per hour, I chose to take the impact through the bumper of a parked car. My right knee took the primary hit, tearing three out of four ligaments and forming three deadly embolisms. My head and neck took the secondary impact as I landed.

Everything's going dark.

I was unconscious for over an hour.

Sweet God, who are you?

I asked this to the face of a Special Forces Ranger Medic who was ministering to me and telling me that my helmet had cracked in half.

Because I was stationed at a base with only a clinic and no hospital, I was treated for a small femur fracture and ordered to bedrest.

I wish that were the end of my accident story.

Chapter 6
I'm in Trouble

The most visible injury, after initial assessment of my accident, was my femur fracture. Although the break was just a couple of inches, the doctor was astonishingly clear to me when he explained that it takes at least two thousand pounds of pressure to break the human femur! That fact put the severity of my injury into context.

Why is my lower leg starting to look so dark?

There was nothing I could do about that break at the time. My leg was so swollen and bruised, the doctor thought it would be dangerous to cast it. I'm glad he insisted on that decision! During the next week when I started physical therapy, I remember my doctor appeared. The therapist was concerned with my condition due to the increased swelling and color of my lower leg. Telltale signs of gangrene presented themselves: I lost circulation in my lower right leg, and my ankle had swollen to nearly fourteen inches. As my doctor searched for pulses in my leg and foot, he found none below my knee.

Before I knew it, I was in an ambulance headed to Winn Army Hospital at Ft. Stewart. The hour-long ride between Army bases seemed endless. It was my first ride in an ambulance, and I had no real idea what was going on. I was only eighteen and not much was making sense. I just knew my leg looked funny and hurt a lot.

When I arrived at the hospital, I was on a gurney, and the doctor was speaking about something with urgency. He was saying, "Compartment syndrome. We need to test for compartment syndrome, compartment syndrome." They did some painful tests and determined I had three large blood clots. Because I was young and knew nothing about the severity of my condition, I had little understanding of the situation I faced. Instead, I wasn't taking things too seriously, hopping around on one leg, trying to get to the bathroom and moving around. My doctor was furious with me. He put a medical book in front of my nose and told me to read about what I had: DVT, deep vein thrombosis.

I'm in trouble!

I spent almost nine months in the hospital. When I was told they wanted to perform an above-the-knee amputation, the gravity of my injuries hit me with more force than running my motorcycle into the back of a parked car at forty miles an hour.

With that pronouncement, God gained my undivided attention.

Lord Jesus, son of God, have mercy on me.

Yes, I made a bargain with God to save my leg.

I promise to serve you, God.

Fearing my blood clots created a real risk, doctors decided to treat me heavily with antibiotics to battle the infection. My bargain with the Lord worked.

Thank you. Deo gratias.

Chapter 7
I Always Keep A Promise

But keeping this promise took more than three years. After my lengthy hospitalization and rehab, I was retired from the Army on medical disability. The gravity of my injuries, especially the blood clots and the traumatic brain injury (TBI), was not that clear to me at the time. I was only a nineteen-year-old.

OMG, these headaches!

So much attention was given to my blood clots and leg function and so little attention given to the impact my head took, the impact that cracked my helmet in two. There had to be consequences, right? What if I hadn't been wearing a helmet? That would have been my skull instead! But since the doctors were mostly focused on the clots, so was I.

But my headaches were unrelenting, bringing tears to my eyes almost daily. Everyone has headaches, right? Were mine normal?

Suck it up, buttercup.

Along with extreme headaches, I had mood swings and bouts of forgetfulness. But my leg worried me more. I had to watch for those darn clots. Never mind the brain. I thought it would take care of itself. To this day, there are events in time surrounding my accident that I cannot recall

Now, to my blood clot injury and traumatic brain injury, add post-traumatic amnesia.

Trying to ignore it all, I dabbled with college courses and played my guitar until I felt I could no longer ignore the promise I made to the Lord for saving me.

Are you still there, Lord?

Chapter 8
Grateful To Be Alive

Three and a half years after my departure from the U.S. Army and two broken engagements later, I donned another uniform. I entered a convent in Boston, Massachusetts, The Daughters of St. Paul, as a pre-postulant. I continued there until the end of my novitiate and prepared to take first vows as a "junior professed," meaning I was able to renew my vows yearly for five years with the freedom to leave before final profession.

A year and a half after entering the convent and five years after my serious incident, I visited the scene of my motorcycle accident.

Te Deum Laudamus.

Diana de Avila at the site of her motorcycle accident

Chapter 9
What's Happening to My Eyesight?

A year after I entered the convent, doctors discovered that I suffered from optic neuritis. Very few specialists recognized it, and at the time, optic neuritis was never explored as being a sign of what was later to be diagnosed as multiple sclerosis.

Benedicamus Domino. What's happening to my eyesight?

I dealt with the condition nearly the whole time I was at The Daughters of St. Paul.

While I was in Boston with The Daughters of St. Paul, my heart was seeking other suitors. I had been in touch with various communities and longed to live as a contemplative, the spiritual focus of the Carmelite Order within the Catholic Church. I wanted to be a contemplative in order to devote myself to unceasing prayer and to wear the Carmelite habit, just like my favorite saint, St. Therese of Lisieux.

The director of novices at the time detected my inner search and interpreted my restlessness as a sign that I was not meant for religious life. She noticed my increasing anxiety as I was approaching first vows. I was looking at all my options, but surely, I didn't expect what happened next.

You don't believe I am cut out for religious life, Mother Superior?

I left, heartbroken. After nearly five years in the convent where I worked primarily in the book bindery, operating and fixing the various Heidelberg binding machines, I felt lost again.

I had been raised in a wonderfully close family with five siblings, including three brothers and two sisters, my twin brother and I being the youngest. My mom was especially religious. Of all my siblings, I was the only one to follow in her spiritual footsteps. My desire to live a life of service and to give back was modeled by my mom, as well as my maternal grandparents. That was the primary reason why I joined the Army. That was why I entered the convent. My leaving both of these noble groups was not voluntary.

Can I find meaning somewhere again?

Chapter 10
All A's for the First Time

I can't believe it! I'm getting all A's for the first time in my life.

I never thought I was cut out for college. Aside from my desire to serve my country, my mediocre high school grades were one of the reasons that caused me to consider the Army. I didn't want to waste anyone's money just to try out college. I really felt I had to do some maturing first.

After leaving The Daughters of St. Paul, I knew I was not ready to give up my religious vocation. I entered a Franciscan community in Cherry Hill, New Jersey that required I finish a two-year degree before entering.

I had three literature classes left to take, and at the age of twenty-eight, I finally learned how to learn. I got straight A's for the first time in my life!

I entered the Franciscan community with my new associate degree. The sisters encouraged me to continue on for a four-year degree to eventually teach or become a social worker. In opposition to my experience in high school, I thrived in college and earned a stellar record until Mother Superior spoke.

You must be kidding, Mother Superior!

She did not approve of my perfect grades and happiness in achieving them because she deemed it prideful.

Really?

Terribly conflicted but out of obedience, I stopped turning in assignments, perplexing my professors. These actions added to my growing internal conundrum. I still graduated magna cum laude but with no family in attendance nor even one sister present to congratulate me.

After three years of stress, I was unmistakably miserable. Other signs began emerging of what was eventually diagnosed as multiple sclerosis, although doctors at the time still weren't looking for a neurological disease. I was convinced that if I didn't leave, I would only get sicker, emotionally and physically.

Once again, I spoke to the Mother Superior and told her my plight. In the austere way this particular community operated at the time, she shouted at me, "You'll never be happy, and you'll be back. But make sure you're gone by tomorrow morning."

Thrown out of my own house.

Chapter 11
Time to Start Fresh

Lay life again, Dee. You can do this.

I packed my car and took myself and the last three years of my seven-year convent life back to upstate New York and the comfort of my lay family.

Time to start fresh.

I felt no need to find another religious community to join and serve, but I wrestled in my dreams about my still unsatiated desire to serve. I dabbled in temporary work, sang in an operatic choir, and looked at graduate schools.

Damn my knee!

Due to my disability and walking issues (though MS had yet to be diagnosed), I decided on a small school rather than one with a large state campus that would be physically unmanageable.

Hey, I like this flyer with the ying-yang symbol.

I chose The College of Saint Rose in Albany, New York. My major was School Psychology simply because I liked their flyer. In college again, I loved statistical and analytical work and focused on post-traumatic stress disorder (PTSD) among military veterans. Looking back, I realize how cutting-edge St. Rose's courses were and how little thought I gave to deciding on a major.

But I'm not stopping now.

Chapter 12
Have I Learned Anything?

What do you think about this, Mother Superior?

I earned my Master of Science in Education (M.S.Ed.) degree with honors. Before applying for a school psych job, I first considered doctoral programs in counseling psychology.

I hoped to stay local due to my unpredictable health, but when the program I wanted most passed me over for the only open spot it had, I stopped pursuing that path.

Damn, I heard they gave that one spot to a professor's daughter.

Deflated, I turned away from thoughts of further, formal education, just as I later stopped pursuing a career with the FBI while on my search for a life of meaning and service.

Have I learned anything?

While life is neither fair nor predictable, it can be fun, just as it was growing up, being close to my twin brother and being the tomboy that I was most comfortable being. I searched for joy, and I started playing a Celtic snare drum with a police bagpipe and drum band. We marched in Ireland and participated in parades throughout upper New York State.

Whoa, I can't feel my legs.

Within four years of being in the band, my MS was still undiagnosed, but it had become impossible for me to march longer than a mile.

At the same time that I joined the band, I also joined New York's version of the National Guard, entering as a captain and psychologist. I even wished my disability retirement would allow me back in the Army as an officer now that I had a graduate degree.

What fun to serve again.

Chapter 13
Some Things Are Not Meant To Be

My life was comforting, and because I had figured out how to learn and be a stellar student, I was accepted into a doctoral program. However, I took to the computer and trends in technology instead, even teaching myself to code over a couple of years. Not only did I love it, I was damn good at it!

Shush, Mother Superior. I am not being prideful, just honest.

Yearning for new excitement and expanded joy again, I applied for a job completely out of the psychology field as an internet technical producer for an entertainment company in Albany, New York. Being knee-deep into technology and working in a creative environment with musical artists, creating web pages and preparing chat sessions for them, was exhilarating. It was the dot-com era, and creative uses of technology were exploding.

Headhunters called. There was a huge need for my skills. What an opportunity and another high point in my career! I felt so good about myself and what I had accomplished despite my brain injury and chronic medical issues resulting from it.

Sorry, Mother Superior. Not really.

Hey, what's this newspaper ad? "Web Architect needed at GE Corporate Research?"

After GE's nine-month search for the right person, they hired me! I was ecstatic; they believed

I had great potential with a long career runway.

I passed my Six Sigma Black Belt certification, enjoyed what I was doing working on a project called Single Sign-on with international partners. Life was good until something new began happening.

What's going on with my hands?

A hand specialist sent me for electromyography (EMG) muscle testing and steroid shots. He felt something neurological might be going on, not carpal tunnel. He suggested I see a neurologist.

I didn't.

It took six months of pain and braces for the pain to subside. Then, a short time later, everything changed again.

Oh, boy, what's this massive headache behind my right eye?

Chapter 14
God, Give Me Strength

The orthopedic hand surgeon who wanted me to see a neurologist was going to get his wish.

Within an hour of my massive headache, my eyesight started to dim, and I lost acuity. I became legally blind.

Was this incident related to my eye problems when I was back in the convent?

I visited with a top neurologist who focused on multiple sclerosis (MS), but my eye did not heal. I was put on temporary disability from GE for five weeks.

Another journey begins. God, give me strength.

Within three days of returning to my job and the work I loved, my other eye became affected.

Now what?

Visual field testing, other testing? What more do I need to go through?

The official MS diagnosis came right after those tests, and the doctor and I discussed what medication I would start.

Copaxone?

Doctors worked hard to stabilize my condition, which took a year of juggling medications, optic neuritis, and doctor's appointments.

Sadly, I had to retire early from what I had thought was my dream job.

During that medical-appointment-filled year, I had flashbacks to my muscle weakness and fatigue in basic training detected even before my accident in the Army; to my eye problems when in the convent; to the trouble I had marching in the police band; to the pain in my hands at GE; to more optic neuritis; to new bladder, gut, and internal issues.

Dear God, how long have I had MS without realizing it?

Chapter 15
Something Wonderful

You've got to be kidding me!

The following year, I learned that Fort McClellan was deemed a toxic town. During my time at Fort McClellan, until it was closed, the Army base had housed and disposed of chemical weapons. Chemical waste leached into the soil and water supply. The community was compensated, but not the soldiers.

Does everything always happen for a reason?

Stage IV endometriosis caught up with me, plus adhesions in my gut that led to a frozen abdomen. The necessary hysterectomy lasted five hours.

But, out of all this, something wonderful happened, as well.

It was love at first sight. Thank you, God, for answering my prayers.

After graduate school and transient romantic relationships, I prayed that I would finally meet someone. Someone who shared my faith, was smart, and had a sense of humor. I was seeking a best friend and a spiritual sister (even if I did not know it as fully back then). I met CC and our bond was instantaneous. Another prayer answered. I was renewed!

Once the MS was relatively stable, with CC working on graduate studies in political science and by my side, we started an import/export business in luxury jeans and other commercial products which were hot

We invented a little pouch for carrying an asthma inhaler, naming it the Med Ready Puffer Tote, and manufactured thirty thousand of them! We were busy!

Jeans and coca tea were added to our product list. After selling about seven thousand of our totes, we donated the rest to a charity in Australia where the rate of childhood asthma was one of the highest in the world. But the stress of operating a high production business took its toll on me, causing my MS to flare.

Chapter 16
Not Ready for What Came Next

Do I have any more parts of me to be removed?

For the next two years, we offloaded our products and sold our huge stash of denim, as doctors and surgeries plagued me. Thyroid. Gallbladder. Appendix. And my remaining ovary. (I had begged the doctor to leave me one when the hysterectomy was performed.)

I wasn't ready for what happened next.

Dad's gone. Oh, God, no.

Dad's first colonoscopy was also his last. He waited too long. It was rectal cancer. The sadness and stress of losing him, even though we hadn't always agreed with each other, caused my MS to flare yet again.

With no more import/export business, no dad, and fewer original, internal parts left to me, I continued the search for meaning and joy.

Dad, I hope you'd be proud of me following in your footsteps.

I like my call sign: W2NU. Whiskey-Two-November-Uniform.

I received my amateur radio license and passed through the three levels, helped give technician classes, and became a volunteer examiner. I finally understood more fully why my dad loved his electronics.

I have a great ham shack, Dad, and I remember you with every communication.

Chapter 17
I Still Want To Serve

The need to serve led me to follow yet another interest. I became an emergency medical technician (EMT). I rode the ambulance until physical demands became too difficult. Then, I helped teach EMT classes. My self-taught information technology (IT) experience enabled me to become the station's geek, bringing iPads to the rigs for patient records and redoing the entire station!

Hmm, am I trying to fulfill that earlier desire as a just-turned-eighteen-year-old to serve others, now in a medical capacity?

Done with school, the love of my life longed for an academic job, and I longed for the sun. We moved to the Gulf Coast of Florida. I was happy. CC was not, initially, but a satisfying teaching position came along after a few years.

Other than going to the James A. Haley Tampa VA Hospital for annual spinal cord visits requiring a short hospital stay, life was good. My MS was stable. And I was ever grateful.

Mom, we'd love to have you here.

*

Cha-ching! Mom moved, and she and I made great sales on eBay.

When Mom joined us in Florida, we found tremendous joy in joining forces and hunting for eBay items at the local Goodwill stores. We were both very routinized, and our eBay jaunts became as much a part of our schedules as dinner time.

During the days while CC was teaching, we would hunt for goodies to flip on eBay: from vintage glass to vintage jewelry. Stores around us were chock full of treasures, if you knew what you were looking for. We made a handsome profit. I had been dealing in glass but was having issues with shipping, handling, and breakage. When six beautiful vintage champagne glasses succumbed to a crush injury, the time had come to pivot and find something that was easier to ship.

Jeans! I knew luxury jeans, and one point about them in particular: local stores had an almost endless supply. "Jean Hunter" was born, and I was turning my $4.50 investments into $29.99 with every sale. At the height of my business venture, I had over six hundred pairs categorized by size and brand ready to ship. On average, I was shipping out six pairs a day and getting into my groove. I loved the challenge and versatility!

Playing on eBay with Mom made for great memories. I loved having her so near again. We'd always been close, and I so admired her strength and spirit. Mom was the woman I looked up to literally and figuratively. She stood 5'10" and always had a wonderfully elegant air about her. As a kid, I loved to be by her side shopping and running errands. Coming home from school often meant a mammoth supermarket visit with our large family to feed or shopping at the Goodwill.

Mom loved to dream and always saw life as filled with legions of possibility and adventure. Those dreams often became reality, and, growing up in a large family, we lived a special life filled with various entrepreneurial ventures where everyone pitched in.

My somewhat risk-averse dad could rarely, if ever, say no to Mom. Their love and respect for each other provided a perfect model for us. So, when she decided to move to Florida, it was totally natural to give her a warm welcome from cold New York winters. A couple of years raced by in relative joy and calm with Mom in Florida.

With Mom still with me (*thank you, Lord*) during the spring of 2017, the calm was disrupted.

My world began to spin. Literally.

Help me, Lord.

Chapter 18
Intense Vertigo

Intense vertigo overwhelmed me. I had never shied away from challenges, but this one catapulted me way out of my comfort zone.

I need help!

At first, the doctor dismissed my vertigo. A week later, at the same doctor's office, we discovered one of my hearing aid cones was stuck in my ear.

Did that misplaced cone contribute to my spinning world?

The doctor laughed at my question and immediately became my ex-doctor.

I felt tipsy and off balance, walking into door jambs. Had I not been diagnosed with MS, I might have mistaken those manifestations for a stroke.

Two days after that appointment, I could bear it no longer.

Please, get me to the hospital. Please, stop the pain in my right eye.

My vision steadily worsened, and hospital personnel thought I really was having a stroke. After collaborating with my VA neurologist, doctors decided on high dose steroids (one gram per day), the normal protocol for an MS exacerbation of optic neuritis.

I've been at this juncture many times before.

Three days of steroids. One gram a day for three days. Typical. On the fourth day, I was sent home with a two-week oral steroid taper needed by the adrenal gland and released to a neuro-ophthalmologist's care.

Weird. I'm feeling a little crazier this time around from the steroids.

Chapter 19
Moment of My Awakening

I *can almost put my finger on the moment it happened.*

It being my awakening, the arrival of what experts have called my "accidental genius."

On a warm evening in late June 2017, just days after getting home from the hospital stay and exacerbation of my MS and optic neuritis, the Depo-Medrol I was taking had left a tell-tale metallic taste in my mouth. I had always used lemon drop candies in the past to mask that persistent taste, but those candies hardly provided reprieve for the taste that night. That metallic taste was a sobering reminder of a part of my personal history difficult to ignore: multiple sclerosis.

I'm still grateful, God.

Even before that incredible evening in late June, my life had been full enough. Interesting in ways that make lives gratifying for those willing to step away from the norm and out of their comfort zone. I loved pushing the envelope of life experience. And I never let myself feel sorry for my lot in life.

Hey, Pollyanna, don't start now.

But I had never experienced anything like this ever!

Because MS loved to go after my eyesight, I was often treated with large doses of steroids. A steroid taper was supposed to lessen side effects. Tapering was not only supposed to make the side effects less intense, but make my anxiety and agitation more bearable.

I was doing exactly what I normally did in those circumstances: two weeks of a gradual steroid taper to stave off side effects and compulsions. For me, abatement had become routine but as important as actual treatment. Without a slow and predictable subsiding of steroids, life could temporarily feel like a psychotic mess.

That evening, I recalled trigger reflexes, responses, and anxiety. I decided to go for a swim and remembered seeing a menagerie of colors, a kaleidoscope of sorts, sitting right in front of my nose. I squinted my eyes the same way you squeeze them when you've looked at the sun just a bit too long.

I squeezed them shut, opened them wide, squeezed them shut, opened them again.

Nope, colors are still there.

Is this what they mean when they say sometimes things just come out of the blue?

Chapter 20
I Want to Create

I got out of the pool, dried myself and felt different. Very, very different. I experienced a brand new, never-before-known compulsion.

I wanted to create something.

Colors were still swimming right in front of me. These colors, these shapes were begging me to exist in the real world. Begging me to translate from my head to something more material in the here and now, in the real world where we all exist.

I don't understand it. Will these colors and shapes go away?

They wouldn't. They demanded an audience, and I became the leader of their band. I sat at my computer. It was the only place I could think of to get these colors and shapes out of my head.

Illustrators use software programs, so let me look.

No matter that I did not know how to use them, I downloaded the software to my computer.

Let's start there, anyway. I don't understand what's happening but I have no choice.

A frenzy of colors and shapes appeared that June evening. They constituted "my awakening," and they harmonized with my uncontrollable compulsion to generate from them at that moment and the days, months, and years that have followed. At that time, however, I had no understanding of the origins of my desire and aptitude.

Have I been struck by a lightning bolt?

I had to let this creativity emerge. And I had downloaded the tools I thought would help, even though I had no clue how to use them.

Just start.

Chapter 21

Blobs Circles Boomerangs

My digital art began with a stylus moving across the tablet. The simplicity and primitive shapes of that first art are almost symbolic of an artist being born. I had to create designs. I felt little choice in the matter. Compulsion and necessity reigned.

The urgency to create that struck me that summer night has immersed me every day since.

This is fun! Hey, what I can do is pretty cool.

I thrived getting the odd and colorful shapes out of my head. My stylus moved smoothly as I devised flowing lines with rhythm and movement. I knew nothing about art concepts. I don't know what overtook me and caused me to make such strange and colorful blobs, but it was the first instance of my surprising gift.

I spent a few weeks playing daily with blobs and boomerangs, and then felt drawn to experiment anew. But where to go for inspiration?

Cats. That's where to go. I love my cats and cats in general.

My favorite cartoon cat was the Pink Panther. We had rescue cats, and the prince of the brood was a little orange tabby cat named Ozzy, with midget features. He was like his own cartoon character.

I can still see you, Ozzy, though you are long gone.

But that didn't matter. I created a little Ozzy cartoon cat. Ozzy had been cool, and he needed Ray-Bans. I obliged.

These cats were comforting and fun, like a downshift after weeks of other shapes and sounds, but I couldn't get these voices of color out of my head: white, teal, orange, brown.

After a few weeks with my cool cats, my compulsion turned to abstraction, and colors and shapes emerged. I needed to bring my artistic satisfaction to a new level. It seemed the only way to quiet the voices of color. These colors, both accessible and comforting to me, resembled the design aesthetic found in the Eames atomic, mid-century style of the 1940s - 1960s that I had taken a shine to over the last few years. (The space-age images were named for artist, architect, and designer Ray-Bernice Eames in partnership with her husband Charles Eames.) Perhaps my love of mid-century modern art led me to see these colors as my first abstract work.

Colors spinning as shapes, again demanding expression. Creamy white for negative space. Brown for slender parts from top to bottom; and circles became orange that brought more comfort.

What's all this about comfort and resolve?

Chapter 22
Digital for Keeps

Since 2017 and the arrival of my gift, I have found comfort and resolve only when I can move the colors and shapes out of my head and into the world.

It's the same with sounds I hear when creating art. Their music quells the constant ringing in my ears due to my TBI. Oddly, I can hear the sounds of art, making me feel as if these vibrations and tonality are coming from my brain and not my ears.

I never dreamed about being an artist growing up.

In fact, I was never even slightly interested in visual arts, nor did I know much about the field. I never took an art class, an art lesson, or an art appreciation class. I never sat with a sketchbook, looking for subjects to draw or paint. And I hadn't a clue about what an art show was, let alone a juried exhibition.

Where's my guitar and drums?

I had loved singing in a choir and playing an instrument. That's where my aesthetics resided when I was younger. Always highly left-brained (analytical and methodical), I was surprised to find art on my radar. That is, until mid-year in 2017.

How did I get rewired? I never could and still can't draw.

Even affixing my name on an identification tag was a telltale sign that my writing was messy. Something else was driving my compulsion to create. Almost as if it wasn't me. Some other energy grabbed my hand and mouse and guided it along the path of dozens of graphics programs to express itself in shapes. I was never scared. Each creation invigorated me to create another and find out what it would be.

Is this art? What's going on with me?

I was prolifically producing, all the while enjoying my digital art yet never ever having had a lesson in art. This fact is still true today.

Blobs, cats, a brief and unsatisfying excursion into abstractions with acrylics and paintbrushes, all were part of my artistic marathon.

Simultaneously to my work with blobs, abstractions and cats, I tried acrylic paints and palette knives, thinking that an artist had to employ a physical medium. I ended up destroying almost all of them, leaving little evidence of their existence except for two, some photos, and a small dropcloth I used. The acrylics on canvas did not feel intuitive or natural for me. All I felt when I tried using them was that I was wasting a lot of good paint!

I remember shopping for art supplies and filling my cart with all the equipment an artist might use, only to give those art materials away soon after.

After dabbling with acrylics on canvas, I went digital by the fall of 2017.

Good-bye, physical paints! Good-bye palette knives!

Chapter 23
It's Pouring Out of Me

Hmm, *fractals are fun.*

Instead of paints, brushes, and palette knives, I "upshifted" to fractal software. Upshifted is my term for delving into manipulations of more complex processes using multiple software applications and mathematical concepts in the creation of my art.

I began working with the fractal concept of self-similarity (though I had little idea of everything these processes entailed when I began). Yet I was drawn to fractal manipulations and always returned to them after short excursions and experiments with fewer manipulations, "downshifts" as I came to call them. These downshifts in my art processes included the series I created with cats, birds, and flowers as subject matter. I also made forays into the creation of pop art.

Time and again, however, I returned to fractals. For the uninitiated, fractals are dynamic systems of highly complex patterns of self-similarities created in feedback loops.

The perfect fractal concept of self-similarity is visible in one of my favorite works of my art, *Drippy Metal*, as shown on the next page. The finished image reminds me of metal tentacles.

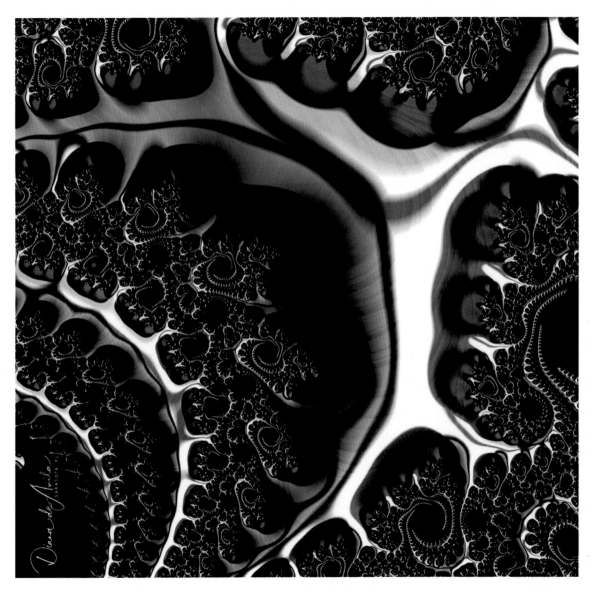

Drippy Metal

A classic fractal swirl with perfect self-similarity, *Industrial Nautilus* was one of the first pieces I sold. The buyer requested it be printed on metal.

Fractals were fast becoming my preferred and favorite manipulation and were soon followed by working with millions of quadratic Bezier curves. Bezier curves are curved lines defined by control points in the world of vector graphics.

Winter Hush

*W*inter Hush is a fractal manipulation, capturing a fractal in the natural world. This particular image is of an evergreen touched by snow. I felt as if I were lying on my back peering up through the trees at an impressive, beautiful moon. This was my first attempt at capturing a fractal in nature through fractal manipulation.

What makes me so prolific and compulsive? What makes me feel so rewarded by this gift bestowed upon me through the unlikeliest of circumstances?

Chapter 24
Is There Anybody Out There Like Me?

When I wasn't producing my art, I spent considerable time researching possible origins of my sudden ability. My need to understand my new gift led me to Dr. Darold Treffert and the Agnesian Healthcare's Treffert Center in Fond du Lac, Wisconsin two-and-one-half years after my awakening and after producing over one thousand pieces.

Dr. Treffert investigated the kind of phenomena I felt I was experiencing. Not only was Dr. Treffert an expert in acquired savant syndrome, he was also an expert on those born as autistic savants. In fact, he consulted during the making of the movie *Rainman*, which won four Academy Awards and was based on the character of a real autistic savant named Kim Peek.

This leading expert in sudden acquired skills that were the result of a traumatic brain injury, Dr. Treffert, became my hope for an explanation. I wrote him in early January of 2020:

Dear Dr. Treffert,

My name is Diana de Avila, and I live in Sarasota, FL. In June of 2017, I had an MS relapse and worsening TBI, which left me in a manic state after three days of high dose steroids and two weeks of taper.

Visions of colors and shapes appeared right in front of me along with a weird desire and compulsion to create art. I'm not an artist, and I can't really draw, so all this was very strange. It happened so suddenly, and I am at a loss to explain.

I have read that people who have brain injury or stroke can suddenly develop these amazing abilities. I feel as if that has happened to me. I am attaching my website, a couple of local TV interviews, and a newspaper interview for you to review.

I don't know what I should be doing with this information. What should I do next? Where do I go? Is there anybody out there like me?

Sincerely,

Diana de Avila

OMG. He responded.

First, however, I received a kind note from his assistant, whom I later discovered was his daughter, acknowledging receipt of my desperate inquiry and reassuring me that my email was being forwarded to the team and to be patient while awaiting a reply.

Fortunately, I did not have to wait long. Within a day of receiving the note from Dr. Treffert's assistant, Dr. Treffert wrote me:

Diana,

Your letter to the Treffert Center was referred to me. I reviewed your bio, artwork, and video clip. Your story is compelling and your artwork amazing. Your story reminds me a lot of Jason Padgett from his book *Struck by Genius*, even though his dormant talent was math rather than art. But the new synesthesia he experienced was very similar to your awakening. May I share your experience with Maureen Seaburg who wrote the book with Jason and is an expert in synesthesia?

I appreciate having your story and artwork available. I do get requests regarding acquired savants and would like to add you to our registry with your permission. You can review some of my writings on acquired savant syndrome and sudden genius on the www.treffertcenter.com website or at the www.savantsyndrome.com website.

I am in contact with another such artist who is considering starting a Facebook site for other acquired savants to share their experiences with one another. I hope that might come about. Beyond that, I hope someone might do a good documentary on that topic to explore more deeply that amazing phenomenon. You can check out some of my thoughts on the Scientific American 2014 piece on sudden genius or view my TED talk in Fond du Lac by Googling TED talk, Treffert, Fond du Lac, Sudden Genius.

I am not sure where the next step is in distributing information about this extraordinary phenomenon, but I appreciate knowing of your story and artwork. Thanks for sharing. If this note triggers questions, send them on.

Darold A. Treffert, M.D.

Wow! I am not going crazy.

Chapter 25
I'm Not Alone

Was Dr. Treffert describing me in his letter?

Yes, and he was describing only a few hundred others in the world who have, as he says, "pervasive disabilities and prodigious talent." Most of these savants are males.

I spent the next four and a half months creating more digital art, of course, and also searching for other sudden acquired savants. I found one, and one found me, and, excitedly, I wrote to Dr. Treffert again:

Dear Dr. Treffert,

I have been in contact with two male acquired artistic savants, like me, since we were last in contact. We are working together to start a sudden acquired savant syndrome (SASS) artistic collective. I wanted to let you know.

My art has continued to advance since we were in contact several months ago. The learning and process of creating my art seems very intuitive to me, although I still have no idea where that learning and ability came from. But it has been fun.

I've been focusing on my fractal work and have just started to animate some of them. I am finding them relaxing and hypnotic. I've created a video with ambient sounds and music, and created a fractal that looked like the crosscut of a tree. I animated the tree rings, and they are very soothing.

I just wanted to share where my work is heading. It's been a wonderful journey. I'm looking forward to finding more of "us" and building that Collective.

Best wishes. I hope this finds you well.

Diana de Avila

Diana,

Thank you for your message and more samples of your work. Impressive and exciting. The tree rings are hypnotic. Let me know how the SASS effort moves forward. I know a number of acquired savants who would welcome and benefit from such a forum. And it would provide a learning venture for us all. I also think it would bring even more of "us" to attention.

Thanks for your interest and update.

Darold

What encouragement!
I'm going to get this Collective going, Dr. Treffert.
I need a mission for the Collective.

It's right in front of my nose! It's not for us to pose as superior artists in contrast to others who have trained their whole lives for such a career. Wanting to understand is not bragging.

What is the Collective's real purpose? The purpose is rooted in trying to find a community like myself. As Treffert said, there are only about three hundred plus savants, mostly males, some congenital, some acquired, in the world. The purpose of our community is to be witnessed and to understand. And, equally important, this community would encourage anyone, with or without a traumatic brain injury or other challenges, to remain positive about life. The Collective's purpose is also to educate and inspire all of us to never give up.

Thank you, Dr. Treffert, for helping us clarify our mission. Who knows what kind of buried potential is in us all! Forgive me, Mother Superior. I am exhibiting my work! And even a line of clothing with my designs.

I knew nothing about art until my gift appeared. And I knew even less about how art shows worked, let along juried ones. I just went and did it. How exhilarating when my work is accepted or chosen or sold!

Sorry, Mother Superior. Not really.

Chapter 26
All Things Are Possible

I awake each day to create and share.

Constantly experimenting with a bunch of software programs, I found my learning doesn't involve reading manuals or taking tutorials. I let the software interface speak for itself with intuition guiding me.

My way of learning and using software intuitively has made it more difficult to teach anyone what I am doing. I find myself using one piece of software to achieve a look or texture and then passing a piece back and forth between software programs and devices to create something unusual and pleasing. Very few of my art pieces use the same workflow. I create from intuition and obey the colors and shapes in front of me.

Many unanswered questions remain. Did my left-lobe injury cause my right lobe to overcompensate? How could I be simultaneously at peace and yet wholly awakened to this exciting new development? Why, in 2019, two years following my awakening, did I start seeing shapes and visions in 3-D? And why did I start putting some of my art into motion?

Is this really accidental genius?

Will the gift go away? Is it fear that compels me to create so prolifically? While I don't believe I make art out of fear of losing my gift, my inner voice and sudden brainstorms do consume me. Creating as I do gives me solace and surprises as well as sleepless nights, thanks to my TBI and MS.

But I plan to enjoy every moment creating my art and learning more and more about this incredible gift. I can't imagine a life now without creating. Each day bright colors beckon me and my synesthesia-driven brain to bring them to a new digital canvas.

Whenever I think about my life before my awakening in 2017, I realize my artist life is just in its infancy. I've produced almost one thousand pieces as of this writing. I have so much faith in the future of my art.

My blessed life and mysterious gift have inspired me, and, I hope, you, as well. All things are possible.

Avalon

Part II

My Story Through Art

Arrival of My Accidental Genius.

Boomerangs and Blobs

*B*oomerangs and Blobs was my very first piece of art. The act began with a stylus moving across the tablet in early summer of 2017.

This blob art creation marked the first time I was able to move the colorful lights from my head into something concrete. I was creating flowing lines with rhythm and kinetic energy. Not trained in art theory or art history, I did not try to analyze the origins of my new art, but it was the first evidence of my artistic savantism.

Frenetic Fish

I noticed fish-type squiggles starting to appear in some of my pieces. Within a month, some fish squiggles became deliberate. I created about twenty more fish-themed blobs during this time.

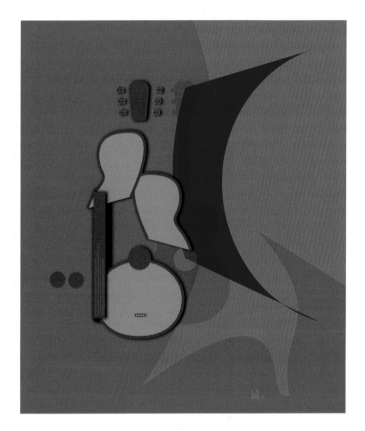

Flamenco

I continued to use shapes and shadowing in my art. *Flamenco* was a first attempt at creating a familiar object with abstraction thrown in.

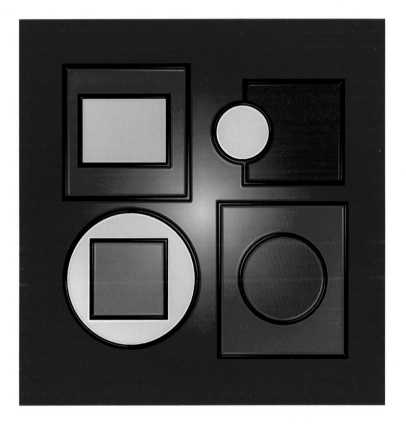

Shape Shifters

During my Blob period, I experimented with software and began to blend processes. This trial and error allowed me to move beyond some of the flat vector creations I made earlier. I thought *Shape Shifters* resembled a sheet of metal. This design felt like a breakthrough as well as an opportunity to add more dimension to my art.

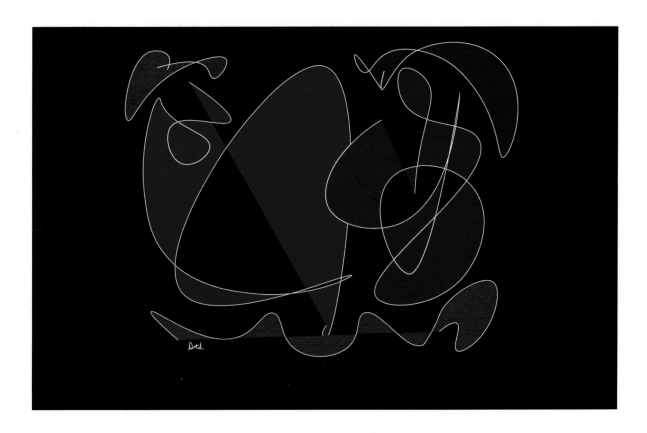

Night Ruminations

*D*ark and peaceful. Color and movement.

Birds in Paradise

My eyesight was going through adjustments during that summer (and still is as I deal with worsening double vision). I tended to favor the brighter colors that came in synesthetic visions. The palette was bright and cheery, like me. More fish squiggles with red dots for eyes. Red dots would become a hallmark, and something I would intentionally begin to add to all my pieces.

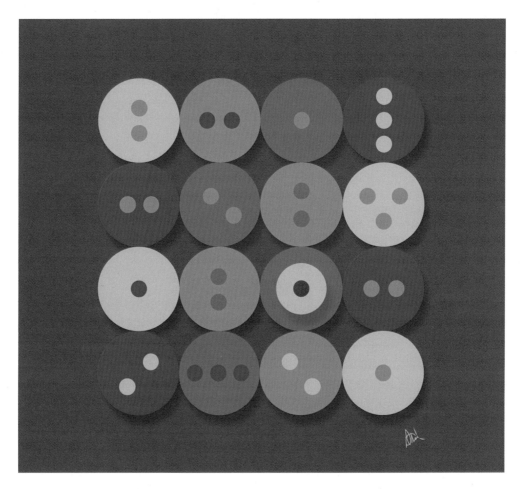

Bullseye

A very prominent red dot. *Bullseye* is the first piece where I intentionally added the red dot.

*B*y August 2017, I left my blobs behind and moved toward something more endearing. *Ozzy Cool Cat* began the short interlude of my *Cool Cats* series.

Ozzy and Hashtags

Here's the first one.

Catabunga

I was having fun with my whimsical *Cool Cats* which were no more than cats' heads. I loved immortalizing all the cats I had known and loved.

Kindergarten Kitty

Any way in which I could incorporate Ozzy made me smile during a time that felt very strange and compulsive. Sometimes the compulsion to create became exhausting. But I was driven to create, and so I did. These *Cool Cats* served as my first diversion from abstract art. It made me giggle, countering my exhaustion.

Cool Cats at the Beach

I thoroughly enjoyed doing *Cool Cats at the Beach*, immortalizing friends' and neighbors' special kitties.

Catbanas on Siesta Key

This final *Cool Cat* piece has gone through several iterations, as I originally created *Catbanas on Siesta Key* for a neighbor with three kitties and was commissioned several times to incorporate different kitties. This piece was also made into a blanket and towels.

I started selling these *Cool Cat* pieces at a local restaurant in Sarasota. The exchange marked the first time anyone ever paid me for my newfound abilities as an artist.

Hatch a Cat

Another special *Cool Cat* piece I made for the local breakfast place that sold my art.

What Lies Beneath

While still experimenting and creating my abstractions and cat art, I made a temporary detour into acrylic paints, believing that artists needed to use palette knives. I ended up destroying most of these acrylic works. One of the few traces of this art remains in the photographs I took.

Digital art became my primary medium by the fall of 2017. Throughout the summer, I was largely imitating what I had known or seen.

Denim

My attempt to use physical paints and palette knives is evidenced in the work *Denim*.

By November 2017, I began working almost exclusively in geometric pieces. In December, I entered my first diptych into a juried show, six months after the arrival of my sudden artistic ability. It was accepted.

Blocked

It was fulfilling to see *Blocked* hanging on a gallery wall.

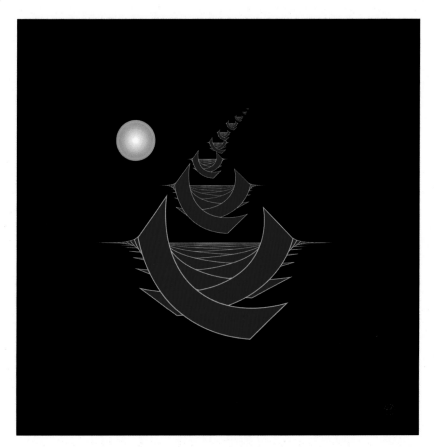

Arabian Nights

I entered this piece into a second juried show in March 2018. *Arabian Nights* landed a great spot in the gallery. This artwork was my take on developing a sense of fractal geometry using self-similarity and scale. I still did not quite understand what I was doing but felt driven to create perspective and scale.

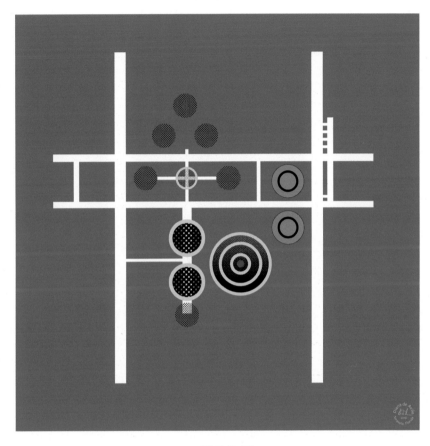

Child's Play

*B*ack to finding solace in my geometric pieces and my red dot with *Child's Play*.

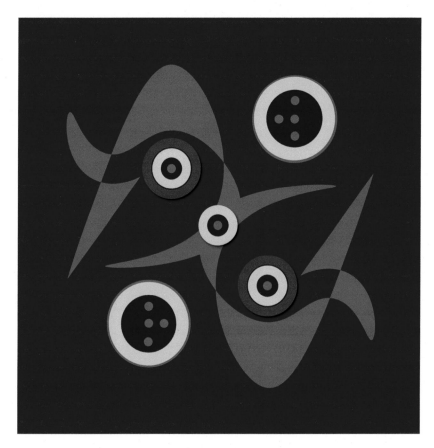

Pip

*B*right colors beckoned to me, and my synesthesia-driven brain wanted to put them on a digital canvas. *Pip* was spinning in my mind, and I could hear the whooshing sound of ball bearings, a sound I heard a lot. The sound even drowned my red dot.

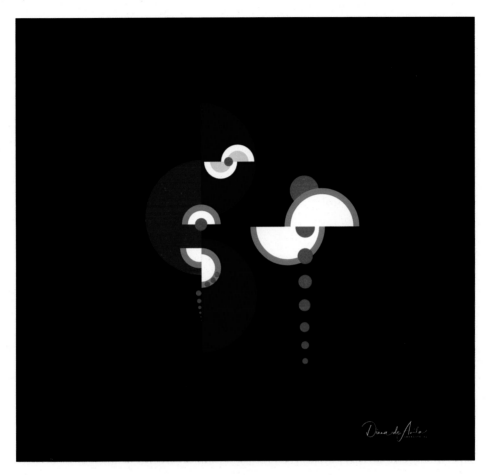

Halves

My signature and artistic identity moved through phases from 2017 through 2019. My red dot began to make it into the initials of my signature as its own little mark.

In 2020, I returned to my simple initials. My artistic identity evolved into a larger ornate vector signature that became part of my artwork.

In 2018, I became The Red Dot Artist for awhile, an identity that I could hide behind, in a way. My red penny (a round seal with initials, a year and my name) became my signature.

I had a web domain and website pointing to this identity, and it was the way I referred to myself. I did not seem ready to launch out on my own yet, unsure that my identity as an artist was enough to carry my work.

In the beginning of 2019, confidence arrived.

Sorry, Mother Superior. Again, not really.

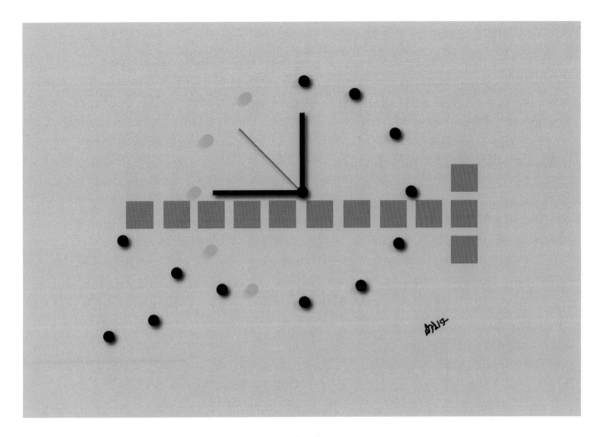

Tik-Tok

Aloss of time and space: *Tik-Tok*, created in late 2017, seems symbolic, in retrospect. In 2018, I created other versions around the concept of lost time. I felt as if I were inhabiting a strange new space in my hyper-reality and seemed to have little understanding of the origin of all those floating shapes and colors.

Everything was very colorful! Time was suspended, and all I felt like I could do during this period was create, create, create.

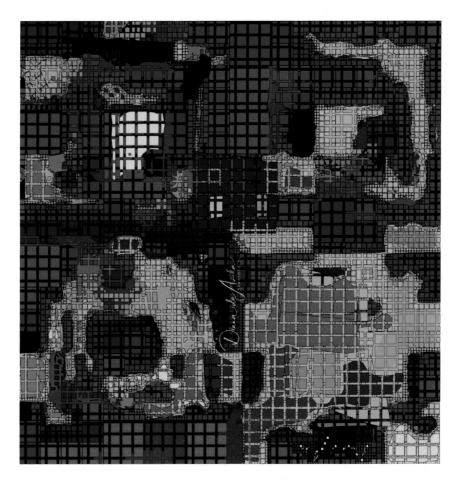

Messing with Rubik

Fractals started making their way out again! Triggered by music I had been playing, I realized I was using the same five or six songs and had them on repeat for almost a full year.

Time flies when you're having fun!

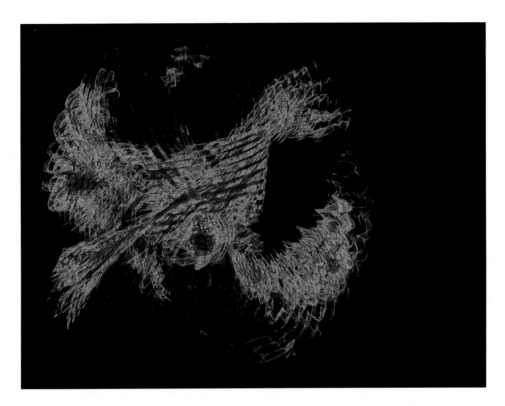

Unnamed

A first fractal flame appeared with no identifying artist's signature. I started experimenting with new software programs to begin to achieve this realm in my art. Unlike most contemporary artists, my artistic work came through a process I did not fully understand. Not being schooled in art or art history, I let the visions in front of my eyes speak and direct my software tools.

My innate processes have made guiding others in how to achieve similar artistic images very difficult. I started to play with various software to create unusual effects. The complexity of using multiple software programs and processes has become integral to how I make art.

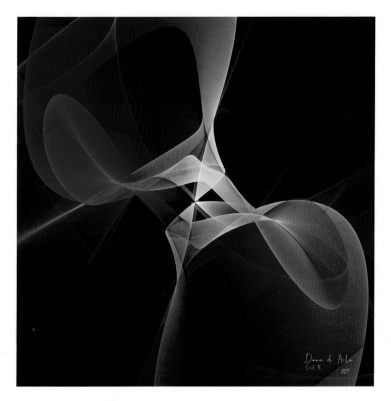

Technicolor Kiss

In June 2018, I entered my work in a third juried exhibition held at the Art Center Sarasota, a Florida-wide competition called *Florida's Finest.* The juror was from The Ringling College of Art and Design. My art was accepted, and I was stoked! My signature red dot was visible in *Technicolor Kiss*, emphasizing that search for my identity as an artist.

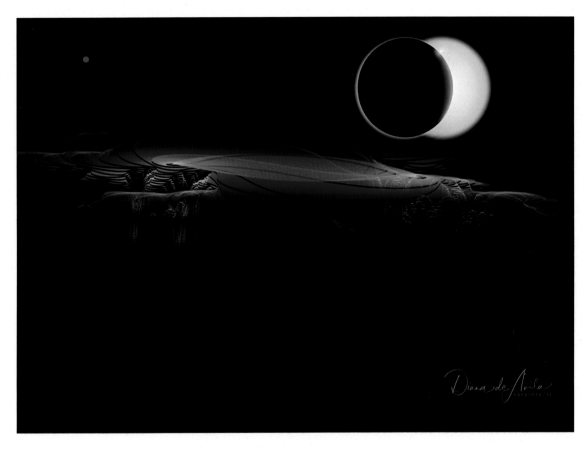

Thion C27

Fractals started taking shape within otherworldly visions. *Thion C27* was based on my visions of a planet with a body of water. During this period, a full year after I became an artist, many of my fractals took on a sci-fi aura.

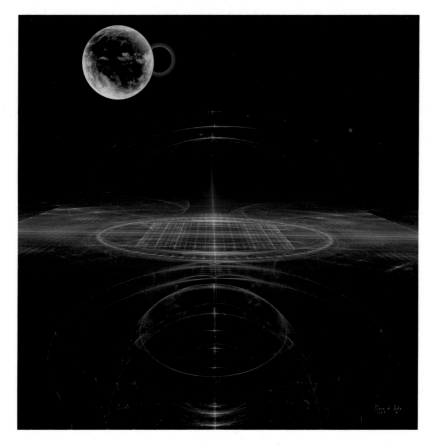

Helipad

By the time I created *Helipad* in 2018, the red dot had become a fixture in my work. I tucked it into each new piece.

Saturn's Bowls

I began adding new elements, such as ball bearings, to my fractal manipulations, as shown in *Saturn's Bowls*. I was now seeing these works in motion and working on finding a way to express movement in the pieces through angles and shadows. I wished others could see and hear those little bearings whizzing around the edge, the way they were in my head.

Avalon

Was I creating my own genre with my fractal manipulations? I didn't know art before this experience. I was recreating what I was seeing in my mind's eye. *Avalon* looked like an otherworldly cathedral or castle made from ice. I loved putting a moon in my manipulations to create a bit of perspective and the illusion of water.

Simple Things

This art is another fractal manipulation designed to capture nature, in this case, a shoreline. *Simple Things* was one of five pieces curated into a special showing in the Veterans Art Gallery at the Virginia War Memorial. The piece was visible in the inaugural *Veterans Art Exhibition* from September 2019 to October 2020. After the show, it was scheduled to be auctioned along with several other works. I donated two of my pieces for their permanent collection.

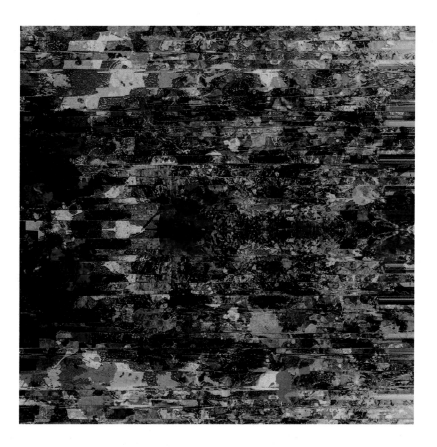

Slice of Life

Apparently, it was time for a short diversion from my working methods again. After creating *Slice of Life*, an abstract piece, I moved away from fractal work for a time. I felt a need to metaphorically downshift from the highly algorithmic and technical art I was producing.

Although slowing down my processes produced some intriguing results, I also realized that leaving my highly technical art processes seemed to last just a few weeks.

Voodoo Triangles

A colorful modern abstract as intriguing digression, *Voodoo Triangles* marked the beginning of my direction toward creating pieces not relying on fractal manipulation.

Glitter Bomb

A strange abstract that arose out of the shapes floating in front of me, *Glitter Bomb* was juried into the exhibition *In Gold We Trust* at the Ashton Gallery in San Diego, California in 2019.

A Modern Interpretation

This abstract originated from my scaled-down processes of creating art. *A Modern Interpretation* was accepted into the Tampa Bay Lightning Foundation's *8th Annual Celebration of the Arts* in September 2019. This regional competition was juried by curators from the Dali Museum and Tampa Museum of Art.

My Mechanized Mind

I enjoyed creating this machine-like abstract. I could see pieces in motion, pushing and pulling.

Brainstormed

Creating the title for *Brainstormed* amused me, as do many of my pieces. I want my art to have personality. There's a red dot in this work, as well.

Goldfinch

I manipulated a standard photograph of a goldfinch from Pixabay.com. Although there are multiple software applications involved, my *Goldfinch* art is evidence of what I term downshifting.

No more cats, however. During this period, I worked through a series of bird images, using my own photographs or those from the photo-sharing site, Pixabay.com. The dynamics I was able to achieve pleased me.

Mauve Mockingbird

With *Mauve Mockingbird*, my processes moved beyond fairly simple manipulations of a photograph, using only one process and a limited number of quadrilaterals. I prefer to deconstruct and reconstruct the photograph incorporating manual techniques. Sometimes I create intriguing photorealistic pieces using hundreds of thousands of shapes. I think of this process as displaying entropy, moving towards order.

The deconstruction and reconstruction of *Mauve Mockingbird* from a standard Pixabay.com photograph felt like a new way of creating art. The combination of techniques and software has become my mainstay, setting me apart from other fractal and digital artists. I like to find a way to twist the typical mechanics of a software process and blend it with something unexpected, something atypical: just like me.

Anhinga

I used primitive shapes, in this case quadrilaterals, to begin the process of creating the finished art. This stage shows entropy.

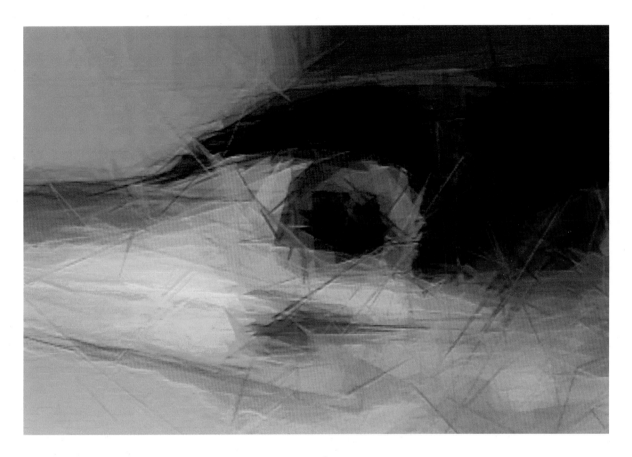

Anhinga

A close up of my Anhinga's eye! This artwork in process began with manipulations of my own photograph of the bird. *Anhinga* is composed of one hundred fifty-one thousand quadrilaterals and a few thousand Bezier curves to add texture. This art-in-stages moves away from the realism of the photograph where it began.

Anhinga

This finished photorealistic digital art was created from a photograph deconstructed then reconstructed from basic shapes. The concept is similar to the idea of the dissectologist, first taking apart the pieces of a puzzle in order to reconstruct an image. I'm not sure why this way of making art from one of my photographs has endeared itself to me, but I find the creative experience as well as the final product particularly pleasing.

Calla Lily

I ventured from birds to flowers in creating news ways to consider subject matter. *Calla Lily* began with one of my favorite photographs of a calla lily, and then I brought in bits of radiance and a little glow. I love working with light and shadows to refine and alter a work.

T his flower is so sweet I could smell it coming off my digital canvas. Creating the series of flowers was very special to me. *Lily of the Valley* started with the raw material of a photograph from Pixabay.com before I drew on software and multiple techniques to create something entirely new and yet familiar.

Of all my works of art, my flower images have been the most widely appreciated. They appear to resonate with a wider audience.

Lily of the Valley

Yellow Selby Orchids

After a few weeks creating flower and bird art, I moved from these worlds into abstracts again. *Yellow Selby Orchids* became a work of my art after I photographed them at Selby Gardens.

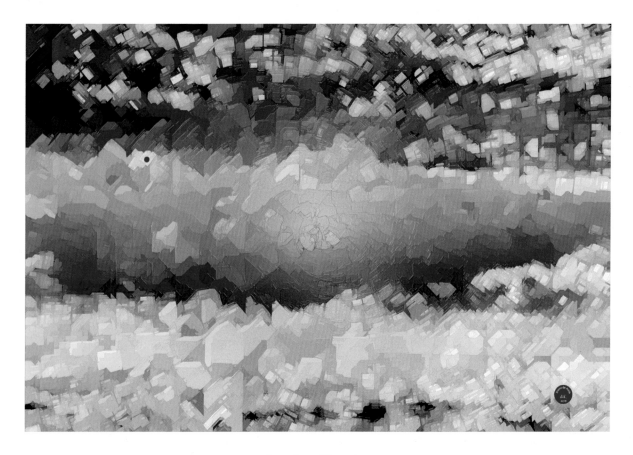

Random Thoughts

Returning from my vacation away from fractals, *Random Thoughts* represents a combination of fractal and photographic manipulations. This work of art was donated to a special pet rescue charity for an auction.

Good Morning Sunshine

Good Morning Sunshine was born as a fractal manipulation that represented a different period for me: a time when I started creating things on a whiter or lighter canvas, starting later in 2019.

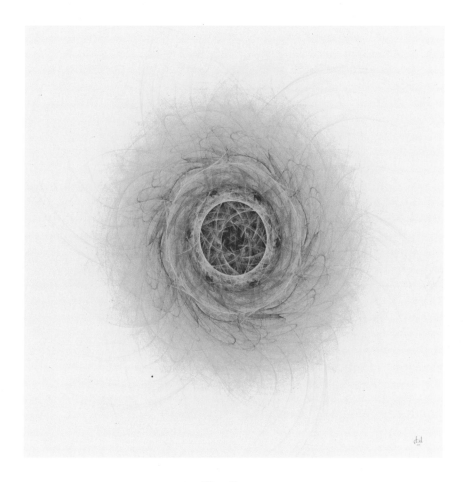

New Spring

A fractal manipulation utilizing tens of thousands of Bezier curves, *New Spring* is one of several of my works created with a lighter palette and background.

Rhapsody in Blue

I felt as if Gershwin himself had created this fractal manipulation for me, and the two fractal figures are dancing in perfect synchrony. The composition played through my head, and naming it was easy. Though an abstract, it is full of movement and delicate beauty. Two ethereal forms danced and flitted through my mind's eye, begging to be documented.

Spectra

Spectra is a fractal manipulation that won a merit award at the Venice Art Center in September 2019 and was entered into a national juried competition at Art Center Sarasota in December 2019.

Pixie Dust

This fractal, *Pixie Dust*, was manipulated in so many different ways, it has almost lost its identity as fractal.

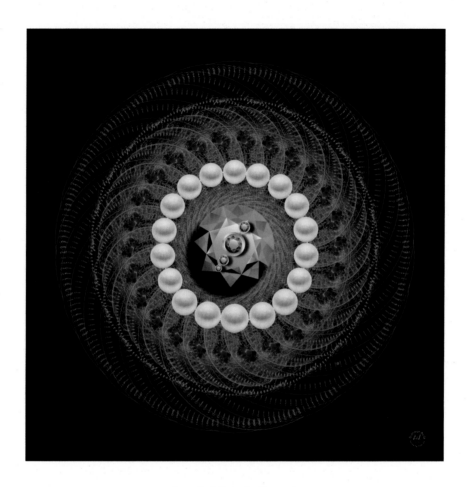

Jeweled Fibula Brooch

One of several fractal manipulations to which I added jeweled elements, *Jeweled Fibula Brooch* appears as if it were a piece of jewelry.

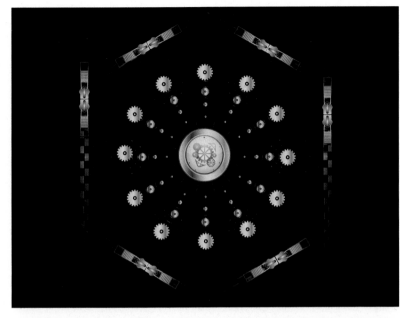

Zipped

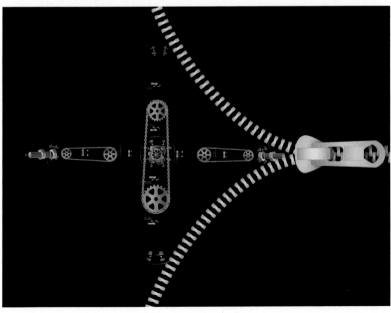

I created a fractal series of four in an industrial theme with gears and zippers.

Cruciform

Whatchamacallit

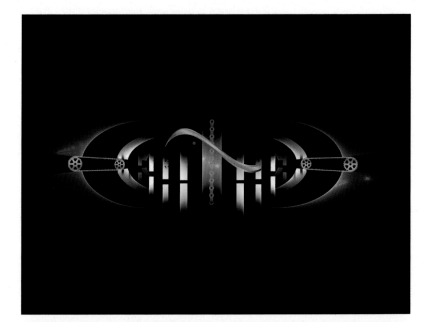

Springee Thingee

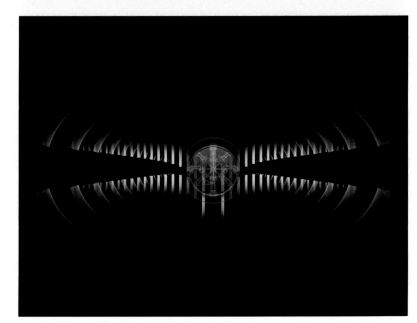

Mindfulness

This mandala fractal was reconstructed from over one million Bezier curves. My artistic companion, the red dot, is the element that brings me back to the beginning of my art journey when it first showed up in my work.

Pools of Light

By 2020, my art started to advance in surprising ways. I moved from imitation to improvisation to creation and found my unique voice. Using elements of light, shimmer, and reflection, I was able to better recreate much of what I was experiencing and visualizing. Art took a new turn for me after I began playing with motion art in mid-2020, after the *Living Tree Insomnia Crusher.* Having spent much time learning new tools and visualizing my synesthetic visions in new ways, I was able to bring my work to an audience closer to the way in which I was seeing it: in motion and in 3D!

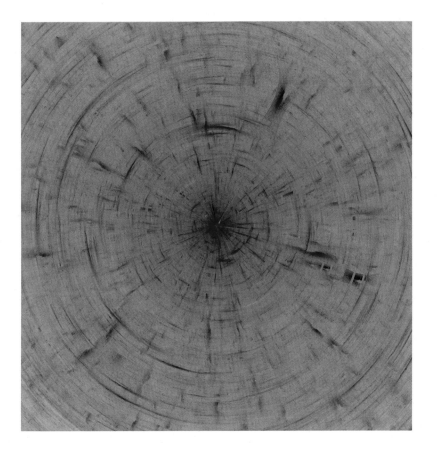

Living Tree

You can see fractals throughout nature. Consider a fractal that looks so much like something you would find in the natural world, it astounds you. When I created this image, or it created itself through me, the art looked like a crosscut of a tree with rings. *Living Tree* could not be visualized in my head without clear, circular movement. The rotational movement soothed me, provided a hypnotic feeling, and made me extremely sleepy. I took things a step further and worked with several variations to form a sequence that was incorporated into my first longer fractal animation. I created it for me, to kill insomnia, but I soon realized this artform could help others.

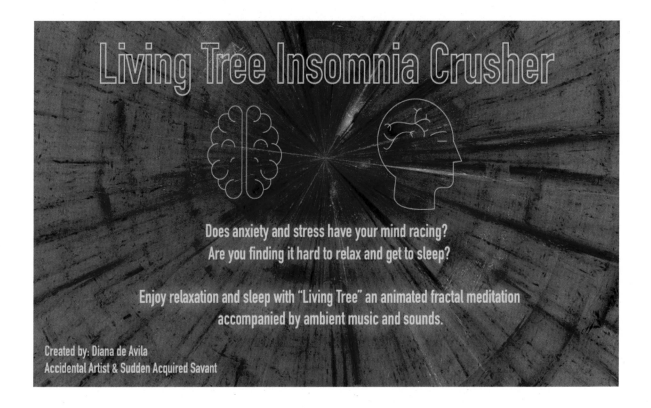

I offered my *Living Tree Insomnia Crusher* on Vimeo for a modest fee. Twenty minutes of spinning tree rings, peaceful music, and nature sounds, this was one of two such relaxation tools I would create. I've always ended up giving far more of them away than I actually sell. That seems a recurring theme with me, considering the special population near and dear to me: my struggling veteran brothers and sisters. Insomnia is a continuing battle I fight as part of my MS and TBI.

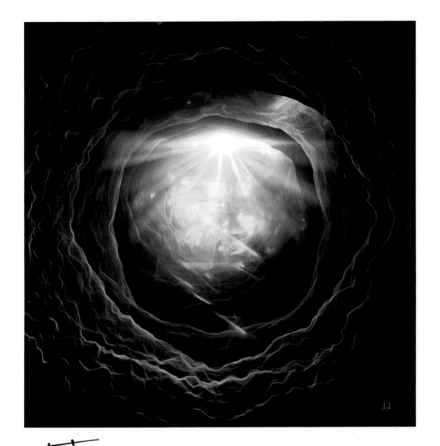

Journey with Morpheus

Journey with Morpheus was driven by an extreme bout of insomnia. In a dazed state, I saw the mouth of a cave, an opening into another world, another consciousness: a life not accessible during wakefulness and not accessible to a neuro-typical individual.

Circular movement and visualization in 3D were some of the driving factors for this piece. Colors reminiscent of Maxfield Parrish with an otherworldly feel, *Journey with Morpheus* feels like a step into a heavenly place, the great beyond, the tunnel of light. The work is comprised of over thirty thousand individual Bezier curves.

13 Thousand Bezier Curves

A fractal created from over thirteen thousand individual Bezier curves, *13 Thousand Bezier Curves* is most aptly named. I love creating art as people have never seen or imagined before.

Having never taken a class or been schooled in art, I have no predisposition as to what is expected of me. I just create what comes through me and what sits in front of my nose. I find the way to get it out of my head. This piece won an award in a national show at Art Center Sarasota in December 2019.

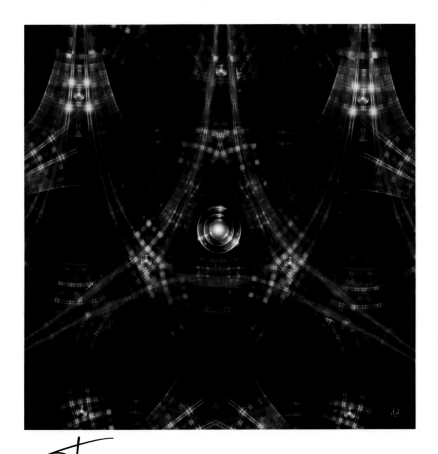

Tour Eiffel

Tour Eiffel is a fractal manipulation created from nearly eight hundred thousand Bezier curves. The art reminded me of the Eiffel Tower lit up with lights. This is actually just one tiny section of the original fractal and is evidence of self-similarity. Sometimes it is a matter of finding a piece of a fractal that represents an object. *Tour Eiffel* is a piece like that.

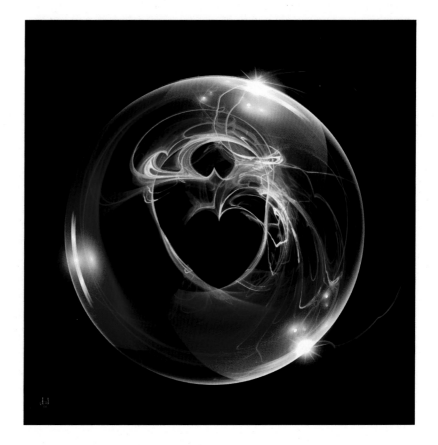

A Guarded Heart

$\mathcal{U}$sing light and reflection, *A Guarded Heart* is a freeform fractal that looks like the outline of an anatomical heart. This heart appears inside a crystal ball or under glass.

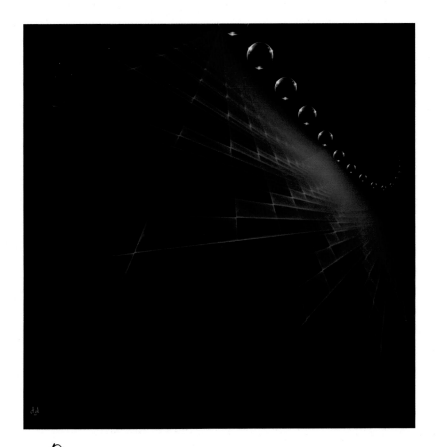

Off the Edge

Off the Edge was created as a fractal manipulation using little crystal spheres and perspective. I saw movement and heard the sound of those little balls rolling across a smooth surface.

The rolling balls' sounds in my head quell the constant ringing in my ears due to my traumatic brain injury. For reasons that are not fully understood, I hear sounds and tones no one else around me can hear even through distractions, such as someone nearby playing the radio or a CD.

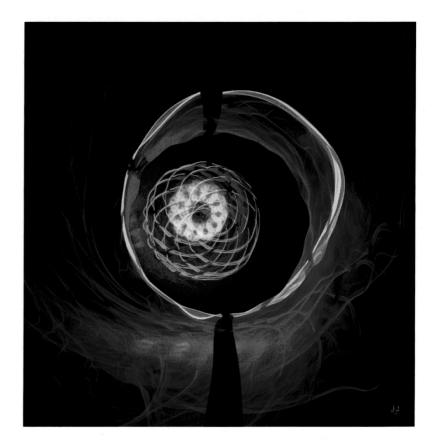

Gravitational Pull

*C*reated from approximately seventy thousand Bezier curves, *Gravitational Pull* was art I saw in motion: orb in the center turning independently from the structure outside it; orb moving clockwise. The outside was moving counterclockwise with a dispersion effect pulling pieces of itself to the center. So much depth!

Hanging By a Thread

*H*anging By a Thread was a fractal that became part of a series utilizing crystal spheres. This one was a prize-winning piece and resembled a chandelier to me.

Antibodies

*G*iven the time of the COVID-19 pandemic, this fractal manipulation arrived and appeared to my inner eye. *Antibodies* felt like an immune system in motion. I was able to put this art in motion, too, and won a special award for the still version in an online exhibition.

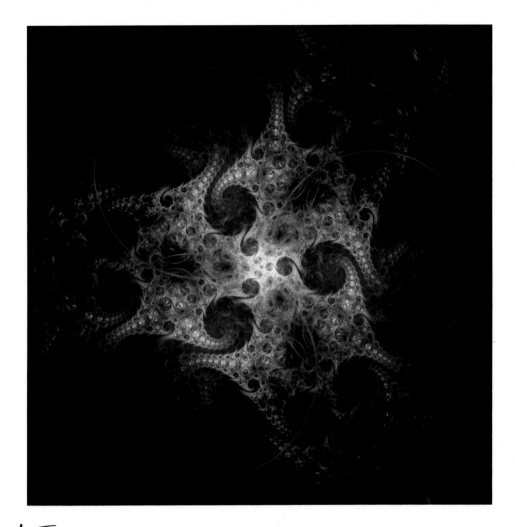

Hydra

This fractal manipulation was created from hundreds of thousands of individual Bezier curves. Look at those tentacles!

Limoges

My *Limoges* fractal manipulation captured the look of gold leaf, cobalt, and Limoges patterns. This particular work of art reminded me of the elegance of a Faberge egg. Many of my fractals have an ornate element to them.

A Strange and Wonderful World

Whimiscal in feel, *A Strange and Wonderful World* is a fractal manipulation that represents an underwater, otherworldly place. My head feels like that. I have also brought this piece into motion with the bubbles rising to the top.

Everlasting Gobstopper

*C*reated from deconstructing and reconstructing a fractal into over one million quadratic Bezier curves, *Everlasting Gobstopper* is the pleasing result.

Zenith

A geometric piece that uses almost two million quadrilaterals, *Zenith* looks like knit fabric. It incorporates my newest signature, which is by far the most indicative of the math inherent in my gift.

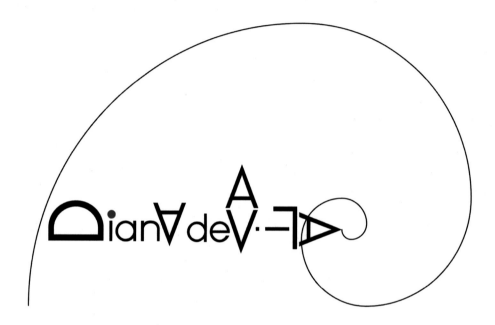

The art here is my newest signature iteration, which encompasses the Golden Ratio. Developed to better express the difference between any two numbers in a sequence, the Golden Ratio is derived from the Fibonacci sequence and is the sum of the two numbers before it. My signature came to me like a synesthetic vision while I was making a smoothie.

This signature is my favorite thus far and best expresses my artistic gift.

A Modern Interpretation & Cicuit

In addition to producing my art on metal, acrylic, and canvas, I am working with a fashion house in Montreal, Canada, which prints my art on dresses, pants, scarves, and other apparel in its clothing line.

Metamorphosis Circa 2017

Photo of me at an art exhibition of my work *Arabian Nights*. Over the last few years, I have experienced the arrival of my sudden artistic skills, and fractals have become my preferred, perfect medium. The fractal allows me to create ornate pieces like *Limoges*, whimsical pieces like *A Strange and Wonderful World*, and geometric pieces like *Off the Edge*. It is as if there are no limits to what I can create using a fractal renderer.

Metamorphosis Circa 2021

Artist and author Diana de Avila carrying *Messing with Rubik*, transformed.

Epilogue

Mom, Ann de Avila

I owe so much to my mom that it makes perfect sense to share her likeness as the last piece of art in this book. She encouraged me from the arrival of my gift in mid-2017. Mom saw the disparity between my using traditional methods with acrylic paints and palette knives and my ability to create art digitally. She witnessed me having to make accommodations for a shaky hand and double vision and recognized that the shift in perception has, ironically, benefitted the way I see my art in layers and 3D. Mom saw that acrylics were not moving at the same accelerated pace as my use of artificial intelligence and manual manipulation.

With her encouragement, I focused on digital art to find my voice. Mom also urged me to hold up my art to the rigors of the acknowledged artist community in Sarasota, Florida. What did I know? I had nothing to lose, right?

The *Mom* portrait also signifies one of my more recent diversions into pop art! So many programs exist to provide overlays and filters on photos. However, using these is not a method I employ as part of my process. Much like my Bezier art, this portrait is a reconstruction from a photo using polygons and moving through various software and devices. I find the look I want and zero in on it. And I never seem to use the same process twice.

Creating this pop art portrait was also the first time since I developed my artistic gifts where I seemed to be able to mechanically work outside my synesthesia. Now I can actually create something on demand. I've done several pop art pieces and have moved beyond relying on synesthesia visions and pure savant inspiration alone. However, it is still more difficult than creating under the guidance of a synesthetic vision.

This act signifies yet a new direction and step in my journey.

It always pays to listen to your mom!

Diana de Avila's Art Exhibitions and Honors

Awards and Honors

❋ 2021, Diana de Avila's acceptance into the National Association of Women Artists, Inc. (NAWA).

❋ 2020, Diana de Avila's acceptance into the National League of American Pen Women (NLAPW).

❋ September 2020, *Journey with Morpheus*, (Award of Excellence and Publicity Award), *The Spirit of Resilience: The Healing Power or Arts and Artists*, Manhattan Arts International, New York, NY.

❋ May 2020 *Antibodies* (Special Recognition), *Art and Vision*, Art Center Sarasota in Sarasota, FL.

❋ February 13, 2020, Featured artist, *Artsy Shark* online feature, artsyshark.com.

❋ January 2020, *Third Eye* (Honorable Mention), *Eye Candy*, Art Center Sarasota, Sarasota, FL.

❋ December 2019, *Hanging by a Thread* (Second Place), *Flashes of Brilliance*, Venice Art Center, Venice, FL.

❋ December 2019, *13 Thousand Bezier Curves* (Special Award), *Open Season* National Juried Competition, Art Center Sarasota, Sarasota, FL.

❋ September 2019 through September 2020, One of 41 Winning Artists, *8th Annual Celebration of the Arts: A Modern Interpretation*, Tampa Bay Lightning Amelie Arena, Tampa Bay, FL.

❋ September 2019, *Spectra* (Merit Award), *Welcome Back to Paradise*, Venice Art Center, Venice, FL.

Juried Exhibitions

❋ April 2021, *13 Thousand Bezier Curves, Hanging by a Thread, and My Mind Wanders, The 49th Annual Melvin Gallery Art National Exhibition*, The Lakeland Art Guild, Lakeland, FL.

❋ March 2021, *Journey with Morpheus, Special Women/Her Story*, National Association of Women Artists, Inc. (NAWA) online exhibition.

❋ October 2020, *Journey with Morpheus and Fractal Sunflower, Onward and Upward*, Art Center Sarasota, Sarasota, FL.

❋ July 2020, *Gravitational Pull, Less is More Exhibition*, Venice Art Center, Venice, FL.

❋ July 2020, *A Strange and Wonderful World, The Big Show: National Juried Exhibition*, Art Center Sarasota, Sarasota, FL.

❋ January 2020, *A Wandering Soul, Untamed: Exhibition*, Venice Art Center, Venice, FL.

Group Exhibitions

❋ May 2021, *New Member Exhibition* , National Association of Women Artists (NAWA), online exhibition.

❋ April 2021, *Bradley | de Avila - Techspressionism Collab No.1*

❋ 2020, *All Members Online Exhibit, ISEA International Society of Experimental Artist*, ISEA - Home (iseaartexhibit.org).

❋ October 2020, *VX 2020, The Center for Global Art*; international online: Center for Global Art | VX 2020 | October.

✤ 2020 *Artscape 2020, Virtual Artists' Market*, Baltimore, MD.

✤ 2020 *Off the Wall*, Art Center Sarasota, Sarasota, FL.

✤ 2019 *Star Spangled Art Exhibit*, St Petersburg College, Tarpon Springs, FL.

✤ 2019-2020 *Inaugural Exhibit, Veterans Art Gallery*, Virginia War Memorial, Richmond, VA.

✤ 2019 *Four Seasons Art Showcase*, MSAA (Multiple Sclerosis Association of America), Art Showcase 2019 - Calling All Artists with MS - MSAA: The Multiple Sclerosis Association Of America (mymsaa.org).

Also by Wilma Davidson

Business Writing: What Works, What Won't (Chinese Edition)

Business Writing: What Works, What Won't (First, Second, and Third Editions)

Most Likely to Succeed at Work: How to Get Ahead Using Everything You Learned in High School
(coathored with Jack Dougherty)

Writing a Winning College Application Essay
(coathored with Susan McCloskey, Ph.D.)

The Bell Labs Editor
(coathored with Richard Trenner)

About the Authors

Wilma Davidson, Ed.D., is a corporate writing and speech coach whose clients have included AT&T Bell Laboratories, Mars Inc., Johnson & Johnson, Anheuser-Busch, and other Fortune 500 companies. She is the president of Davidson & Associates Communications Consultants, and a former faculty member at the University of South Florida. Davidson is the president and a board member of the Sarasota Branch of the National League of American Pen Woman (NLAPW). Wilma Davidson lives in Longboat Key, FL with her husband Steve and spent many years as an instrument-rated private pilot. But that's another story!

Diana de Avila, M.S.Ed., is a disabled U.S. Army veteran who developed extraordinary artistic abilities after a traumatic brain injury and the onset of multiple sclerosis. She is a prolific and award-winning digital artist who previously worked as a web architect for a Fortune 500 company and as an entrepreneur before making the decision to work fulltime on her art. *Soldier, Sister, Savant* is her story. She lives in Osprey, FL. Diana de Avila is a member of the Sarasota Branch of the NLAPW and a juried art member of the National Association of Women Artists (NAWA).